PET CARE LIBRARY

Caring for Your Dog

by Derek Zobel

BELLWETHER MEDIA • MINNEAPOLIS, MN

Note to Librarians, Teachers, and Parents:

Blastoff! Readers are carefully developed by literacy experts and combine standards-based content with developmentally appropriate text.

Level 1 provides the most support through repetition of high-frequency words, light text, predictable sentence patterns, and strong visual support.

Level 2 offers early readers a bit more challenge through varied simple sentences, increased text load, and less repetition of high-frequency words.

Level 3 advances early-fluent readers toward fluency through increased text and concept load, less reliance on visuals, longer sentences, and more literary language.

Level 4 builds reading stamina by providing more text per page, increased use of punctuation, greater variation in sentence patterns, and increasingly challenging vocabulary.

Level 5 encourages children to move from "learning to read" to "reading to learn" by providing even more text, varied writing styles, and less familiar topics.

Whichever book is right for your reader, Blastoff! Readers are the perfect books to build confidence and encourage a love of reading that will last a lifetime!

This edition first published in 2011 by Bellwether Media, Inc.

No part of this publication may be reproduced in whole or in part without written permission of the publisher. For information regarding permission, write to Bellwether Media, Inc., Attention: Permissions Department, 5357 Penn Avenue South, Minneapolis, MN 55419.

Library of Congress Cataloging-in-Publication Data
Zobel, Derek, 1983-
Caring for your dog / by Derek Zobel.
   p. cm. – (Blastoff! readers: Pet care library)
Summary: "Developed by literacy experts for students in grades two through five, this title provides readers with basic information for taking care of dogs"-Provided by publisher.
Includes bibliographical references and index.
ISBN 978-1-60014-466-0 (hardcover : alk. paper)
1. Dogs-Juvenile literature. I. Title.
SF427.Z63 2010
636.7-dc22   2010011390

Printed in the United States of America, North Mankato, MN.
080110   1162

Contents

Choosing a Dog

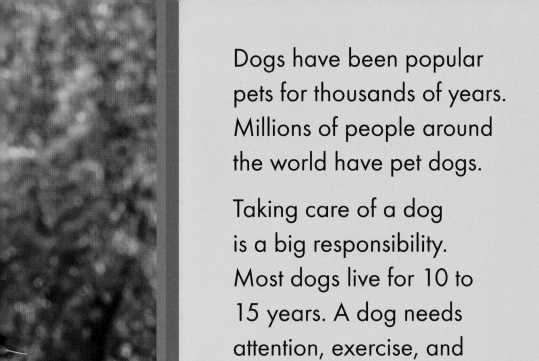

Dogs have been popular pets for thousands of years. Millions of people around the world have pet dogs.

Taking care of a dog is a big responsibility. Most dogs live for 10 to 15 years. A dog needs attention, exercise, and food every day. It also needs shots and regular visits to a **veterinarian**.

! fun fact

Small dogs usually live longer than large dogs. Their bodies don't have to work as hard because they weigh less.

Doberman Pinscher

Pomeranian

Pug

Golden Retriever

There are over 400 dog **breeds** in the world. Every breed has a unique look and different **traits** and behaviors. You will need to choose a breed that has the characteristics you want in a dog.

Many people own **crossbreeds** and **mixed breeds**. These dogs have a combination of traits from different breeds. They also have fewer health problems than **purebred dogs**.

crossbreed

Care Tip

Your dog will feel nervous when you first bring it home. Introduce it to people and other pets slowly. Give it a bed where it can rest comfortably.

You can get your dog from a pet store, **breeder**, or **pet rescue center**. A pet rescue center rescues pets and cares for them until new owners can be found. Wherever you get your dog, you will need supplies from a pet store to properly care for it.

Supply List

Here is a list of supplies you will need to take care of a dog.

- collar with a tag
- grooming brush
- leash
- food and water bowls
- dog food
- dog bed
- dog treats
- dog toys
- kennel

leash

collar with a tag

food bowl

Feeding Your Dog

Care Tip

Dogs like routine. Try to feed your dog around the same times each day.

Dogs are **carnivores**. They like dog food made with meat. Your dog should be fed twice a day and should always have fresh water to drink.

Your dog will beg for treats. Give it dog bones or biscuits for behaving well. Be careful not to give your dog too much human food. Some foods, like chocolate, can make dogs very sick.

House-Training Your Dog

kennel

After your dog eats, it will need to go to the bathroom. Bring your dog outside to prevent it from going inside your house.

Dogs do not like to go to the bathroom where they sleep. Keeping your dog in a **kennel** while you are away helps it learn to wait to go until you take it outside.

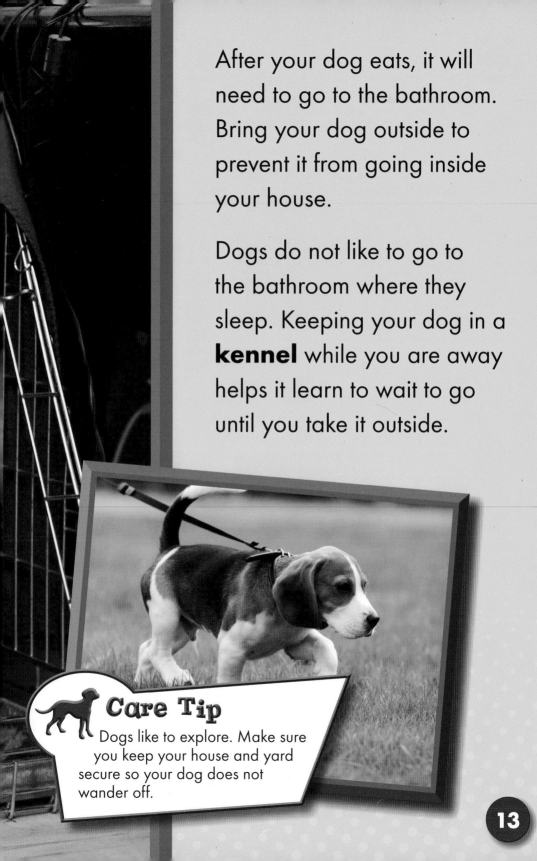

Care Tip

Dogs like to explore. Make sure you keep your house and yard secure so your dog does not wander off.

Grooming, Exercise, and Training

Care Tip
You only need to give your dog a bath once or twice a year unless it likes playing in the mud.

You will need to **groom** your dog. Some dog breeds need regular haircuts to keep their **coats** short. Most dogs **shed** their hair. Brushing your dog a few times a week will keep it from shedding all over your home.

Different dog breeds enjoy different amounts of activity. All dog breeds need some exercise every day.

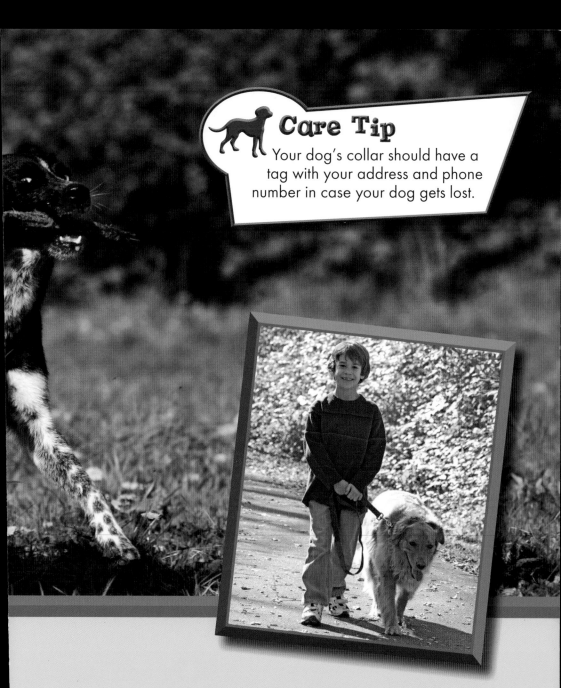

Care Tip

Your dog's collar should have a tag with your address and phone number in case your dog gets lost.

Walk your dog on a leash. You can take it around your neighborhood or even to a **dog park** where it can meet other dogs.

Dogs are very smart. Some are trained to herd animals or help people. Most dogs can learn to play games and do tricks.

Teach your dog to sit, stay, and fetch. Be sure to say your dog's name and reward it with treats. Training your dog will make caring for it much easier.

Keeping Your Dog Healthy

If your dog is not responding to you, not eating, or not moving, it might be sick. You should take it to a veterinarian.

It takes time, effort, and care to develop a bond with your dog. If you can handle the responsibility, you will have a loyal friend for a long time.

Glossary

breeder—a person who raises dogs and sells them to other people

breeds—types of dogs

carnivores—animals that eat meat

coats—the hair or fur of animals

crossbreeds—dogs that are a mix between two breeds

dog park—a park for dogs and their owners

groom—to clean; different breeds of dog require different amounts of grooming.

kennel—a small shelter for a dog; kennels can be used for house-training or traveling.

mixed breeds—dogs that are a mix of more than two breeds

pet rescue center—a place that rescues pets; pet rescue centers care for pets until new owners can be found.

purebred dogs—dogs that are one of the more than 400 recognized dog breeds

shed—to lose; most dog breeds shed their hair.

traits—qualities

veterinarian—a doctor who takes care of animals

To Learn More

AT THE LIBRARY

Foran, Jill. *Caring for Your Dog*. New York, N.Y.: Weigl Publishers, 2003.

Landau, Elaine. *Your Pet Dog*. New York, N.Y.: Children's Press, 2007.

Roca, Núria, and Rosa M. Curto. *Let's Take Care of Our New Dog*. Hauppauge, N.Y.: Barron's Educational, 2006.

ON THE WEB

Learning more about pet care is as easy as 1, 2, 3.

1. Go to www.factsurfer.com.

2. Enter "pet care" into the search box.

3. Click the "Surf" button and you will see a list of related Web sites.

With factsurfer.com, finding more information is just a click away.

Index

The images in this book are reproduced through the courtesy of: East Images, front cover; Sonya Etchison, front cover (small), pp. 16 (small), 17 (small), 20-21; Julija Sapic, pp. 4-5; Nikolai Tsvetkov, p. 6 (top left); Yan Wen, p. 6 (top right); Vivian A Thode, p. 6 (bottom left); Juan Martinez, p. 6 (bottom right), pp. 9 (middle), 15; Alistair Scott/Alamy, p. 7; Paul Shlykov, p. 7 (small, left); Andraž Cerar, p. 7 (small, right); Glow Images, Inc./Photolibrary, pp. 8-9; South 12th Photography, p. 9 (top); Aaron Amat, p. 9 (bottom); Monika Wisniewska, p. 10; Heinz Krimmer/voller Ernst/Photolibrary, p. 11; B Rainer/Age Fotostock, pp. 12-13; Peter Kirillov, p. 13 (small); Maiava Rusden Sri/Photolibrary, p. 14; imagebroker/Alamy, pp. 16-17; Andrew Jankunas/Alamy, pp. 18-19; ableimages/Alamy, p. 19 (small); Corbis/Photolibrary, p. 21.